THE REAL GUIDE TO CONSTRUCTION

BOOKLET 18+

Down-to-Earth Lad

TABLE OF CONTENT

PROLOGUE

This book is for working-class heroes, also known as the "Backbone of Every Country!" This book simplifies construction life with a learning and comedy aspect. Whether you are looking to get into the construction industry, just starting your career in construction, or currently working in construction, this book is for you. If you stick to the advice in this book, you will not go wrong in construction. Do not just read this book once; refer back to it. You may not think this book is useful, but if I had been given this advice when I was a fresh-faced 19 year old going on-site for the first time, I would be much better off now. This book contains information you don't get taught in school or college.

Warning! Contains life-changing advice and explicit language.

This book is about construction life in the UK. Sorry if you're reading this in a warm country, where you get treated fairly and earn good money. Ignore the parts when I talk about cold weather and complain about companies that don't pay enough.
Having no confidence, drinking too much, and hating your job, can lead to mental health concerns. Hopefully, this book can help you realise where you're going wrong and guide you in the right direction. If you're ever feeling down, talk to your workmates and let them know how you're feeling.

Fitness releases endorphins which are a 'feel good' chemical produced by the body. Don't suffer in silence and stay active. This advice is coming from someone who still suffers from mental health issues to this day. My goal for this book is to help prevent you from making the mistakes I made over the years.
We all go through that dreaded feeling of starting a new job, the thought of the unexpected, and the insecurity of 'am I good enough?'
Getting 40 minutes of sleep the night before and worrying about scenarios that may or may not happen is tough. With a good attitude and without trying to please everyone, you can make it in construction. I say, 'without trying to please everyone' because if you try to please everyone, they will take advantage of your softness. There will be times where you need to tell people to 'fuck off.' Construction is a tough environment to work in, and sometimes being nice does not work. It's not very often, but sometimes people need to be put in their place.

Tip: Buy a yellow highlighter pen and highlight parts of this book that will benefit you most.

CHAPTER ONE:

CSCS & NVQ

I don't know what qualifications you need to work on site in other countries, but in the UK you need a CSCS card. If you haven't had a CSCS card before, you will need to do a one day Health and Safety Awareness course. Training centres offer a day course and test packages. (another money making scheme) After doing the course and passing your health and safety test you can then apply for your CSCS green card online. Thankfully you only have to do your CSCS test once every five years

CSCS Card Colours:
Green – Operative/Labourer
Blue- Skilled worker (NVQ Level 2)
Gold – Supervisor (NVQ Level 3)
Black – Management (NVQ Level 6)

An NVQ is a National Vocational Qualification. An NVQ is a work-based qualification that recognises the skills and knowledge of a person to do a job. If you don't have an NVQ, it doesn't mean you're not a skilled worker, although companies like you to have an NVQ to prove that you're qualified and competent. You don't learn anything of value doing your NVQ; if you want to be a skilled worker, just keep turning up and working hard. When I got my NVQ Level 3, the assessor pulled up in his car, asked me to sign my name, and said, "Congratulations, you have passed." He filled in all the answers for me. Maybe it's more professional these days. NVQ assessors' job is to assess the skills you have learnt on-site.

Tip: Get your CSCS card (green)

CHAPTER TWO:
FIRST DAY

Your first day on-site will consist of a site induction which includes: Site Rules, PPE, Muster Point (a safe place to gather if there is a fire), etc.

Try to stay awake for the rest of the induction. Depending on the size of the site, site inductions can take ten minutes or last up to a whole day. Trying to stay focused for a whole day is nearly impossible. I don't know about you, but after 30 minutes of somebody talking, I switch off and start thinking about what I'm going to have for lunch. Once you understand the basic rules of construction, the rest is common sense.

For example, would you walk behind a moving vehicle or wait for the vehicle to pass? Once you have been inducted, you will have to sign a Method Statement, which explains in-depth how to do the job and how to do the job safely. It's normally a few hundred pages long of details to cover the company's arse if something goes wrong. So, they do not get the blame in court. They do not expect you to read the whole Method Statement but have a good flick through and sign away.

Next, you will sign a Risk Assessment. A Risk Assessment assesses a task/situation, breaks down the risks, and identifies ways to reduce them.

For Example: Task - One-nightstand; the risk of pregnancy is 9/10.

How to reduce the risk: Condom or contraceptive pills. The risk is now dramatically reduced to 2/10. A Risk Assessment is about identifying the risk and working out how to reduce that risk as much as possible.

Once you have signed the method statement and risk assessment, you're ready to start work. The site manager or supervisor will show you where to work and what to do. If it is your first time on-site, it can be very daunting, not knowing anyone or not knowing where to go. So, spend some time walking around the site and familiarise yourself with where the canteen is and where the toilets are. Talk to workmates your own age. If you have come from a family background where your mum still tucks you into bed at night, you will find it harder to adapt to construction life. Do not worry about going on-site; we have all been there. Just keep your head down and work hard. Your confidence will come eventually. If you are a site manager, you will not have this problem. "You've been there, done that" and are probably already trying to catch someone out for not wearing a glove whilst they scratch their nose.

The best type of site manager is someone that has come from working with tools and understands what a hard day's work feels like. There are a lot of men/women that come on-site from university, straight into a site management role. It can be hard explaining to someone that you are frustrated and pissed off about working in the rain all day when they don't know how it feels.

Working in construction, you will learn life skills that they don't teach you in school. Forget about all the wasted hours learning about algebra. Welcome to the real world. You will be up early (5/6 AM) and work roughly between 8–10 hours a day.

Depending on your career choice and where you live in the world, you could be working in cold conditions all day. You suddenly start to appreciate the small things in life, like looking forward to a cup of tea.

Tip: Take your CSCS card to the site (you can't be inducted onto the site without your CSCS card)

CHAPTER THREE:

SITE MANAGEMENT

Some site managers will make you work extremely hard to make themselves look better to project managers and other management staff, taking all the credit for your hard work.

Annoying site managers will stand over you whilst you work. There is nothing more annoying than having a clueless manager looking over your shoulder whilst you're trying to work something out.

Good site managers will always be one step ahead, ordering materials to arrive on time, planning for the next day's work, and arranging the best access solution so that you can work safely.

You will be surprised how useless some young managers are. They come straight from university into a management role without any previous site experience. They are easy to spot on-site; they will be walking around the site with a drawing upside down, with a clueless expression on their face, and wearing the cleanest safety boots on-site.

The best type of site manager is someone that has come from working with tools and hasn't forgotten what a hard day's work feels like. A good manager will help you read drawings and tries to help you out as much as possible. If the manager on your site is shit, show him this book, so he knows how to do his job.

Tip: Avoid knobhead/clueless site mangers

CHAPTER FOUR:

CHARACTERS ON-SITE

There are many types of characters on-site (they come in many shapes and sizes); the majority are good, honest, and hard-working people. And then there are the types of people that you need to avoid. I have given the characters you need to avoid nicknames. The names are completely made up or self-explanatory for your entertainment.

The type of people you work with can make a big impact on how your day goes and how much you enjoy working on-site. The best type of person to work with is someone who isn't scared to work hard and can think for themselves.

There will be some people on-site that have most of these characteristics but pick a name that suits them best.

Avoid the characters that I am going to mention now. The type of people you need to work with are true, honest, hard-working men/women that have the initiative to work stuff out for themselves but also work as a team.

There can be a fine line between banter and bullying on-site; just make sure you do not cross the line. Banter is more light-hearted, and bullying is aggressive, personal and harming.

JOBBO

Jobbo:

Someone who is always in and out of the site office cracking jokes with the site managers and basically kissing arse. Jobbo will talk behind your back to site management. Jobbo Works hard when site managers are watching but then goes back to leaning against a wall on his phone. Gullible management staff will believe that Jobbo is a good worker, but if they saw what everyone else sees, they would realise Jobbo is a waste of space.
Jobbo could even go to the extreme of buying management a newspaper or a coffee. Unfortunately, Jobbo type characters can be site managers' favourite
'workers' when true, honest workers get less thought of. Jobbo type characters could go on to be a site manager simply by brown-nosing management staff.

Tip: Avoid Jobbo

JOBBY

Jobby:

Someone who acts like they're busy but is not actually doing much work. Jobby makes a big deal of doing the smallest jobs, puts something in a bin, and wants a medal. When you're working as a team on big projects, you need everyone to play their part and work hard. One person can affect the progression of a job, also known as a Jobby. Jobby prefers being on his phone or standing around talking rather than doing any work.
A Jobby is basically a lazy bastard.

Tip: Avoid Jobby

GOBBY

Gobby:

Someone who talks the talk but cannot walk the walk. Thinks everything is easy but never actually does anything. Gobby has a big mouth and a big ego and doesn't like to be told what to do.

Gobby is basically a big-mouthed knobhead. Gobby never stops talking shit.

When someone is stood back, it's so easy for them to give people advice on how to do a job and how they would do it. Gobby can talk a good job but is useless on the tools.

Tip: Avoid Gobby

GHOST

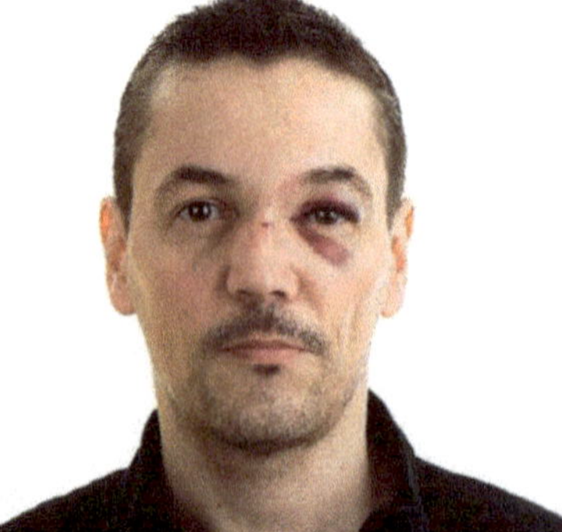

Ghost:

Someone who disappears for hours on end (most likely on their phone in the toilets or in the smoking area). A Ghost character normally disappears towards the end of the day when it is time to clean up and put all the tools away. Ghost is also a member of the Monday club; Monday club is an exclusive club for people who can't make it to work on Mondays.

Monday Club members are highly experienced at thinking on their feet and coming up with excuses as to why they could not make it to work. Monday Club members will deny that they got carried away drinking on Sunday and will come up with excuses like "my goldfish died" or "it was coming out of both ends."

Tip: Avoid Ghost

ASBO

Asbo:

Someone who has the 'inability' to think for themselves, not because they can't but because it's easier to rely on other people. Asbo type characters have a short temper and no manners.

Asbo will rely on you for everything. Asbo characters have been on-site for years, but they are still fucking useless. They will forever be talking and spend most of their day smoking cigarettes in the smoking area.

Asbo will make your stress levels to levels they haven't been to before; he will make you bald with stress.

Tip: Avoid Asbo

WOODY

Woody:

Normally an overweight bald site manager who has nothing good to say; constantly talks absolute bollocks.
"Have you not done that yet?" or "How long will that take" (pull the string from his back, and he will repeat annoying quotes). Woody's have a short temper due to them not being able to run a job properly. They will take their anger out on people working on-site.
Woody will stress you out to the point of wanting to walk off-site. Woody is basically the worst type of site manager.

Tip: Avoid Woody

CHAPTER FIVE:

ROLES ON-SITE

Everyone has a crucial role to play on-site. If you have no qualifications and it is your first time on-site, you're starting off from the very bottom as a labourer/apprentice. Labouring includes tidying up and helping trades move materials, and basically does the job no one else particularly wants to do. If you're keen enough and want to learn, you might have the opportunity to learn a trade. Some people are quite happy being a labourer, there is no stress of building something wrong, or being behind with the project schedule. The only downside is the rate of pay. If you are coming from college to site, you should be on the tools learning from day one. There is only so much you can learn in college, although you have some skills you still have a lot more to learn. Everyone must serve their time, just because you can put in a screw in a wall doesn't mean you are a joiner. Working with fully experienced tradesmen/women you will learn the tricks of the trade—how to read site drawings, set out a building, and the quickest way to drink a pint of beer. Supervisors are responsible for looking after people, making sure people are working safely, and doing the job right. Supervisors should have served their time on the tools to then pass on their experience to the next generation. Not all managers are "Woody" characters, there are some good site managers out there.

Tip: Play your role.

CHAPTER SIX:

EXPERIENCE AND TRUST

Every construction company is looking for experienced workers, but how do you get experience in the first place? People think experience is how long someone has done a job for. I know men that have been working on-site for thirty years, but I still wouldn't trust them to put up a picture frame in my house. The only way to gain experience is by working with other skilled workers and learning from your mistakes (nobody's perfect; we all make mistakes).

An experienced worker is full of knowledge and knows everything there is to know about their trade. An experienced worker does not need to work hard. They can simply walk around the site showing people how to do the job right. A skilled worker is still working hard and learning daily. By having the willingness to learn, the initiative to think for yourself and the willingness to work hard, you will soon be a skilled worker.

The Steps:

- Complete novice learns from skilled workers.
- Skilled workers learn from Experienced workers.

Timescale:

- Novice to skilled worker: 2 - 5 years
- Novice to experienced worker: 10 – 15 years.
- This, of course, depends on the trade.

Trust

There must be a certain level of trust on-site; trusting somebody to do the job right. Real trust can only be earned over time; do not trust anyone you don't know. I would like to say I trust people that I have worked with for a long time but unfortunately, I have worked with Jobby, Jobbo and Gobby type characters.
In the past, I have told a "trustworthy" work mate personal information in complete confidence they would not repeat it to anyone. Before I knew it, everybody on-site knew about what we discussed. This a good method to figure out who your true mates are on-site. If you cannot trust somebody, why would you associate with them, knowing they could grass you up or talk behind your back.

Tip: Don't trust certain people

CHAPTER SEVEN:

THE SETUP

Construction is all about your setup. Preparing/setting out materials and creating a good setup and system will increase your productivity massively. Take ten minutes in the morning to think about the best/easiest way to do a job. Always have your essential tools on you; always have a tape measure and Stanley knife in your pocket. Don't get stressed out trying to find where you have put your tools; always have them nearby. As you get more experienced, you will learn the tricks of the trade and the easiest way to do certain jobs.

Tip: If you don't prepare, prepare to fail

CHAPTER EIGHT:

TO ALL BUSINESS OWNERS AND MANAGERS

The second you stop appreciating hard working people that work for you is the second you become an absolute C***t. The people that get up every day at five in the morning to work hard for you are the reason you have a business. Stay down to earth, and don't forget how important good workers are for your business.

If you treat your workers fairly, they will respect you more and ultimately work harder.

Pay good workers the money they deserve, give them a bonus at Christmas, buy them company T-shirts and put them on training courses. Simple!

Tip: Treat your workers fairly

CHAPTER NINE:

DRINKING

We all know going out for a pint after work is right up there with the invention of electricity, but unlike electricity, drinking can be hard to turn off. The first sip of the first pint can be almost orgasmic; for some people, it's hard knowing when to stop.

As you get older, hangovers get worse. I prefer to go out on a Friday, so I have two days to recover before work on Monday. I was off work one Monday because I was out on a Friday, dying in bed for three days.

So, just know your limits. Do not lay in bed all day feeling sorry for yourself. Take a shower and drink loads of water. One of the reasons for hangovers is dehydration, so make sure you drink lots of water after getting drunk. We all love a beer, but it's knowing when to drink and how much to drink. If you are working on a Saturday, going out on a Friday after work for a couple of beers is fine. But if you're still doing shots at three in the morning, that is when you know you have a problem. I have been out on a weekday, and before I know it, I am in a shitty bar, having a dance-off whilst still wearing my work clothes. The feeling of waking up the next morning, still in your work clothes, with thirty missed calls from your boss, is one of the most sickening feelings. If you put drinking before your job, you will not have a job for long.

Christmas parties can get very messy too. Just keep in mind that you have got to see your work colleagues again. Getting too drunk and acting like a complete dickhead will lead to a very embarrassing walk into work on Monday morning.

For me, the worst part is not remembering what I did. For all I know, I could have been giving the project manager a lap dance.

If you're ever feeling down due to the loss of a family member or you have had a bad day, drinking is not the answer. Alcohol is a depressant; the more you drink, the more you can feel down. Although temporarily alcohol helps you feel good and helps you forget about your problems, you will only feel worse the next day. I used to drink when I had a bad day at work as a self-destructive method. Drinking too much as a self-harm method has the ability to completely ruin your life.
Picture yourself getting up early, having a shower, and feeling ready for the day ahead, to waking up with a mouth like the Sahara Desert, covered in sick and trying to remember what happened the night before. Which start to the day would you choose?

Tip: If you have no limits, do not drink on a weeknight.

CHAPTER TEN:

GOSSIP

Let's be honest there are different skill levels on-site and different qualities of work depending on experience; some people have an eye for detail, and some people can barely see. Grassing/Snitching on somebody for how bad their work is will only backfire! Do not worry about other people's work. Just concentrate on your work and gradually improve your quality. Only bring up someone's shoddy workmanship if it is going to affect your work. For example, if you are a bricklayer and you come to a corner that someone else has already built (badly), you are obviously not going to carry laying bricks, just let someone know that it's not right but never mention someone's name. If that fails and the person responsible for building the leaning tower of Pisa confronts you about refusing to continue with their work, just repeat after me, "fuck off and do your job right next time." Everyone loves a bit of gossip and banter on-site. It's what gets us through the day "did you see Dave fall over before" but calling someone behind their back should never happen.
Every day is a learning day, but if you are a snitch, every day will end with a black eye.

Tip: Do not talk behind someone's back. (Don't be a grass).

CHAPTER ELEVEN:

COMMUNICATION

Communication on-site is the most important factor. A construction-site relies on communication; getting the right information across to the right people can be the difference between a job getting done right and on time. If you're good with people and communication, a management role could be for you. If there was no communication on-site, there would be a site full of people looking around scratching their heads. Information is passed on down by the design team, down to the manufacturing/supplier team, to the on-site management team then onto site operatives. If there is a miss communication between anyone, it can affect the project quality or progression. A simple miscommunication can have devastating effects, for example, houses being built in the wrong colour brick or a banksman telling the crane driver to go up on his line instead of down.

Tip: Communicate and listen.

CHAPTER TWELVE: PATIENCE

Keeping a cool head on-site without reacting aggressively whilst under pressure is so important; letting the pressure get to you will lead to you hating your job and making mistakes. Losing your patience can come from having really high expectations for yourself and others, except the way people are and don't get so stressed about things that don't matter. There have been times when I've walked off-site either when I make a silly mistake, or I'm working with a complete knobhead. Allowing your personal life to affect your life on-site is unhealthy. For example, taking your anger out on your workmates because you have had an argument with a family member. Working with people who have the inability to think for themselves and rely on you for everything can be so stressful, especially when they get paid the same; keeping your cool can sometimes be very hard if you're working with knobheads.

Tip: Keep your cool and avoid knobheads.

CHAPTER THIRTEEN:

PPE AND WORKWEAR

Especially if you are working in cold conditions, having good warm work clothes is so important. By not wearing warm and dry workwear, you will spend half of your time wrapped up in a bed full of Flu. You will spend most of your days wearing your work clothes, so investing in good workwear is key. If you are willing to pay £50 for a pair of jeans that you will hardly ever wear, how much would you pay for a pair of work trousers that you will wear all day, every day? There is nothing worse than being wet and cold all day. Call me old fashioned, but I like wearing a High Vis vest that actually fits me. I prefer to buy my own High Vis because, for some reason, companies only order XXXL or XXXXL sizes. I'm 6 foot tall and weigh 65kg, so you can imagine what an XXXXL High Vis looks like on me. It can also be dangerous to wear clothing that does not fit right. If you're climbing up a scaffold, it can get caught on scaffold clips. What a way to go, cause of death: Oversized Hi-Viz vest. You can buy a decent High Viz vest on Amazon for roughly £10, and they come in all different sizes, with pockets and somewhere to keep your site pass. Gloves are a big thing on-site; they are either skin-tight or really loose. A little tip is to have two pairs of gloves; always keep one pair dry for the next day. A good way to judge a company is how reluctant they are about giving out gloves. If you ask Woody for a pair of gloves and he looks at you like you have just asked to marry his daughter, you are working for someone that isn't really bothered about your welfare. Buy a KASK Plasma safety helmet for all day comfort. Depending on the site, site operatives wear white helmets, and management/supervisors wear black safety helmets.

Tip: Buy good workwear.

CHAPTER FOURTEEN:

KNOWING WHEN

Knowing when to tell people to "fuck off."

When Woody wants you to:

- work unsafe
- put work before your personal life
- take on extra work with no additional pay
- stay in accommodation (Digs) that you wouldn't let your dog stay in
- do more work even though you haven't stopped all day
- work with a knobhead

I do not want to be responsible for you losing your job, so when I say tell Woody to "fuck off," you don't have to say "fuck off." You can word it differently. Just simply refuse to do what he has told you to do. Earlier in the book, I talk about having patience; if you bottle in your emotions, you will eventually explode. Sometimes people need to be told! If you don't tell people to fuck off, they will treat you unfairly. Site managers and company owners will try their luck to try to save pennies and cut corners.

Tip: Fuck off Woody.

CHAPTER FIFTEEN:

COMPANIES TO WORK FOR

Finding a company that puts you first is rare these days. There are a lot of companies that are run by money-driven assholes. A company that will put you through training courses and will have patience whist you learn your trade or further your career are like needles in haystacks. When you finally find a down to earth boss that appreciates you, who can have a laugh with and pays you well, you should never leave him. Avoid working for agencies. Although they source jobs and always pay on time, they take a big cut of your wage. For example, the agency will charge the subcontractor £20 p/h but only pay you £9 p/h. Agency staff sit on their arse all day whilst you work in the cold all day.

Tip: Stay with companies that you enjoy working for. Don't work for agencies.

CHAPTER SIXTEEN:

INVEST

This is no bullshit self-help book, but investing in your future, it will eventually pay off. Especially if you are just starting off in construction, gradually adding to your tool bag and buying the right tools for the trade you have chosen is the best way you can improve your career prospects and earn more money. What use is a joiner without a saw? Going on training courses will also increase your chance of employment and wage increase, build up qualifications for your CV to the point where an employer would be stupid to not give you a job.

Investing in yourself by buying tools and having a willingness to learn can be the difference between earning, for example, £350 a week and earning £500 a week. If you haven't done so already, get yourself a driving licence and a van/car. Some sites may be in the middle of nowhere, so having a van/car is a must unless you like getting three buses at five in the morning.

Tip: Build up your tool collection and qualifications.

CHAPTER SEVENTEEN:
WORK ETHICS

Work ethic can depend on your situation; if you work for yourself, then obviously, you're going to work hard. The more work you get done, the more money you earn. If you are working for a company that you enjoy working for, your work ethic and drive will be high too. If, on the other hand, you are working for a 'Woody' type character, you are naturally going to do as little as possible. The last thing we need in this world is more rich dickheads. Even if you are working for a 'Woody' type character, try to keep up your work ethic whilst applying for other jobs. Do not just walk off-site or risk getting get laid off because now you're losing out on money by being out of work. Depending on where you work in the world, weather conditions can affect your work ethic. You won't be happy working in 40-degree heat or -5 degree cold conditions. Nothing worse than cold, wet hands. The harder you work on-site, the less energy you will have to do stuff out of work, so it's finding the right balance.

Tip: Work hard for the right people.

CHAPTER EIGHTEEN:

HAVING A LIFE

I cannot stress enough that having a life outside construction is so important. If you are getting up, going to work, coming home, making your tea, having a shower, and going straight to bed, this will gradually grind you down to the point you start to hate working. Having something to look forward to will motivate you. For example, remembering that you have a boxing class, a hot date or a holiday booked. Having something to look forward to will put a spring in your step, that feeling of finishing work early on a sunny Friday afternoon to go to the pub. We work hard all year round to provide for our families, save money and go on holidays abroad. Don't get too caught up in work life and forget why you go to work in the first place. Don't forget there is a life outside construction. If all you do is work, life will pass you by, and before you know it, you're a miserable old bastard.

Tip: Don't put work before your life.

CHAPTER NINETEEN:

MONEY

I do not know your financial income or outgoing bills, so really, I should not tell you what to do with your money, but I am going to anyway. If you're the type of person that lives paycheck to paycheck because of your circumstances, that's fine, but if you don't have kids or a wife to spend all your money, putting money away each week and saving for a rainy day is a must.

You never know when you might be out of work or when your car needs a new engine.

Having financial security by having a few thousand in your savings account is also a less stressful life. Especially if you are young and you're seeing money coming into your account for the first it can be very exciting, do not get carried away by getting a car on finance, buying designer clothes, popping champagne on nights out or getting with a partner that expects the finer things in life.

Getting a car on finance can be very exciting, driving around thinking you're a big-time millionaire when in reality you're paying £20,000 for an £11,000 car.

Putting money away as little as £100 a week can soon add up; let's say you work 48 weeks out of the 52 week year. After 48 weeks of saving £100 a week, you will have saved £4,800. That is enough to buy a reliable car or a family holiday.

The amount of money I have spent on stuff that I don't need is ridiculous. Apps like Amazon make it so easy to order online; ask yourself do you actually need it or just want it.

Tip: Save as much money as possible.

HL 55205743
100
ONE HUNDRED DOLLARS

CHAPTER TWENTY:

WORKING AWAY

Working away from home can be great if done right. If your wife/girlfriend doesn't like you going the pub, then working away will give you the freedom to go the pub any night of the week without any stress. If you're lucky enough to be single get yourself out with the locals and mingle.

Working away from home can be great if:
- your accommodation is nice
- you get to go home often
- your paid extra money for working away
- your not working or living with a knobhead

The worst scenario when working away:
- staying in dirty, smelly accommodation
- sharing a room with somebody
- living with a knobhead
- not being able to go home to see your mates/family
- Woody is running the job
- your window cleaner is good looking, and your wife is home alone

Tip: Don't work away from home if your accommodation isn't paid for by your employer

CHAPTER TWENTY-ONE:

TYPES OF EMPLOYMENT AND PAY

Being self-employed will earn you more money and give you a sense of freedom, but you do not get paid whilst you're off work; if you earn £800 a week and you go on holiday for two weeks, you are losing out on £1600 before you have even booked your holiday. You would happily lose out on two weeks' pay because the money companies offer you for being employed directly is embarrassing. Although you get 30 days of paid holiday and a pension scheme, most companies do not pay enough money to live on. Being self-employed and being employed directly can be the difference between renting a two-bedroom house or buying your own four-bedroom house.

UK payment methods:

Day Rate - Paid a set amount for the day (£200 a day)
Paid per hour - Paid for the hours you work (£20 per hour)
Price work - Paid for the amount of work you complete (£20 per square metre)
Per Annum - Amount earned yearly (£20,000)

Tip: Work for a company but be registered self-employed.

CHAPTER TWENTY-TWO:

KNOWING WHEN TO LEAVE A JOB

This is a tough subject to cover. It all depends on your situation and the type of person you are. Here are some reasons why you should consider leaving a site or start working for another company:

- If you are not getting paid the money you deserve
- The commute is too far to travel
- If you constantly get undermined and being spoken down to
- The site is poorly managed.

Not getting paid enough money all comes down to your experience, work ethic and quality of work. The commute to work can add hours to your working day. I would not recommend travelling more than one hour to get to work. If you're being spoken down to by your supervisor or anyone on-site, you need to have a word with them. Ask if they have a problem; no one on-site should experience bullying. Bullies should experience black eyes. A Poorly managed site is a site with bad communication and unsafe working conditions.

Tip: Put yourself first.

CHAPTER TWENTY-THREE:

STARTING YOUR OWN COMPANY

Experience is key when starting your own business. With not enough experience, you will struggle.
Working for a good company is great, but the freedom and financial gain from starting your own business can be extremely rewarding. Starting off small, i.e., employing a young labourer and teaching him the lessons and skills you have learnt. Employing local people that are reliable and willing to learn are the people you need working for you. Also reward the hard-working people you have working for you, i.e., a £100 bonus at Christmas. Build up from there by having good relationships with customers, clients, and employers. If you put your quality of work and customer service first, you will be successful. Have a good accountant. Your accountant will handle all your financial difficulties so you can focus on growing your business. Grow your brand, advertise on social media etc.

Tip: Do not start your own company unless you have at least 10 years of experience working on-site.

To help understand the type of employee you should be, just imagine you're running a company and you need to employ somebody.
Would you employ someone who:

- Never turns up because they're hungover.
- Turns up but is too hungover to work.
- Has no tools to do the job.
- Stands around on their phone.

Or would you employ someone who:

- Turns up on time.
- Has every tool for the job.
- Works hard.

CHAPTER TWENTY-FOUR:

BENEFITS OF WORKING IN CONSTRUCTION

Benefits of working in construction:
- You get to work outdoors and not be stuck in an office environment
- Sense of achievement when producing quality work
- You can earn good money without a university degree
- Unlimited amount of banter
- Keeps you physically fit

There are always simple solutions to the cons in construction. For example: Working in the cold - wear more clothes.

Tip: Don't overcomplicate things; there is always a simple solution.

CHAPTER TWENTY-FIVE:

BASIC HEALTH AND SAFETY INFORMATION

RAMS – Risk Assessments and Method Statements
SPA – Safe Plan of Action
PUWER – Provision and Use of Work Equipment
PPE – Personal Protective Equipment
HASWA – Health and Safety at Work Act
MEWP – Mobile Elevating Work Platforms
COSHH – Control of Substances Hazardous to Health

Biggest Risks in Construction:

- Working at height
- Falls from height
- Adverse weather conditions
- Site Access
- Incorrect PPE
- Moving Vehicles

Thank you for reading this book, and I hope you can learn something from it. This book is short and to the point because, let's be honest, after a hard day's work, the last thing you want to do is read a book; we'd rather be down in the pub.
Keep this book in your bag or in your van, refer back to it for advice and write down notes.
If you're ever feeling down or need advice, whether it be about construction or life in general. I'm offering a completely free advice service to help combat men's mental health in construction, so feel free to give me a message on Instagram @TheRealGuide18

Author: N. Halliday (Down to Earth Lad)

NOTES:

NOTES:

www.ingramcontent.com/pod-product-compliance
Lightning Source LLC
Chambersburg PA
CBHW050014040726
47599CB00014B/1380

* 9 7 8 1 9 1 5 4 2 4 5 6 3 *